Michael J. Murphy was born i
fireman. In 1922 he returned
Armagh and grew up in the
worked as a farm labourer a
life's work as a full-time c
mission. Now retired, he lives with his wife ....
Co. Louth.

Among Michael J. Murphy's other works are: *At Slieve Gullion's Foot*, Dundalgan Press, 1941, *Tyrone Folk Quest*, Blackstaff Press, 1974, and *Ulster Folk of Field and Fireside*, Dundalgan Press, 1983.

MOUNTAIN YEAR

MICHAEL J·MURPHY

illustrated by Wendy Robinson

THE
BLACKSTAFF
PRESS
BELFAST AND WOLFEBORO, NEW HAMPSHIRE

First published in 1964 by
The Dolmen Press Limited

This corrected and illustrated edition published in 1987 by
The Blackstaff Press Limited
3 Galway Park, Dundonald, Belfast BT16 0AN, Northern Ireland
and
27 South Main Street, Wolfeboro, New Hampshire 03894 USA
with the assistance of
The Arts Council of Northern Ireland

Printed in Northern Ireland by
The Universities Press Limited

British Library Cataloguing in Publication Data
Murphy, Michael J. (Michael Joseph), 1913-
Mountain year. — [New ed.]
1. Slieve Gullion (Northern Ireland) —
Description and travel 2. Armagh (Northern
Ireland : County) — Description and travel
I. Title
914.16'6   DA990.S/

Library of Congress Cataloging-in-Publication Data
Murphy, Michael J. (Michael Joseph), 1913-
Mountain year.
1. Murphy, Michael J. (Michael Joseph), 1913-
— Homes and haunts — Northern Ireland — Slieve Gullion.
2. Slieve Gullion (Northern Ireland) — Description and
travel. 3. Armagh (County) — Social life and customs.
4. Authors, Irish — 20th century — Biography. I. Title.
PR6063.U734Z466   1987   828'.91403   [B]   87-11614

ISBN 0 85640 381 4 (hardback)
0 85640 382 2 (paperback)

CONTENTS

I LIVE ON A MOUNTAIN

All my life I had wanted to live on the slope of Slieve Gullion facing south into our end of South Armagh. And I knew why I wanted to live there.

It wasn't for any reason of sentiment. All my people were South Armagh stock from the parish of Dromintee ('Dhrementee' as they said it, which means the *droighneain*, or bushes, of the *sidhe*, or fairies) and since the age of eight I had been living among the South Armagh hills in several houses, but never actually on the mountain itself. In the end it was to become a temple of myth amid encircling acolytes in the hutments of hills; but long before I had known its history and traditions, the earth spirit of Slieve Gullion had begun to draw and even hypnotise me.

I liked the hills from the beginning and had Slieve Gullion in mind when later on I said: 'Three things one should do every year – listen to a storyteller at a fireside, give a hand in a corn harvest field, and climb an Irish mountain.' I climbed the mountain and hills every time I got a chance, on any excuse, even as a boy – to milk goats; to fill sacks with moss for bedding young pigs; to carry burdens of burnt and brittle whin sticks in a rope on my back to provide fuel for making farls of griddle bread.

As boy and man I liked to walk the hills and sit on a high rock, such as one of the two teeth of the Dhaaicklemore on the hill between Armagh and Louth. In a loneliness never silent, in a solitude never still, I would ponder on the sublime rise of Slieve Gullion out of the valleys, on the magnificent dome of the summit which houses the two cairns and the lost, weeping lake. I could look down on the thronging crush of the little fields in the valley; on the whitewashed houses; at a red-leaded, orange farm cart with iron-shod wheels, silent from

1

that height, crawling like a tired beetle along a dusty road; at Garriba ridge and St Patrick's Catholic church perched on top.

And over and out of all I saw and thought, the sense of living quiet whispered and sometimes roared in my mind as if the spirit of the mountain was losing patience in trying to help me understand what it was trying to say. Once or twice, when I was young, I got frightened; but I always went back.

The very sight of a mountain, let alone a remote breath from its personality, can elevate the human spirit by depressing it with that feeling of the mysterious and immense: such a reaction is normal to any level of sensitivity in the human mind. But Slieve Gullion was haunting me at all times, and I wanted to know why it drew me as it did. It had, so to speak, come down as I had grown up, but I believed I could only meet and interpret that spirit if, on level footing, I lived on its slopes myself.

The moods of its personality dominated and influenced the lives and living of everyone within its shadow, even the very fields. Even when I worked in those fields as a half-a-crown-a-day labourer, the spirit of the mountain breathed out of the clay I turned, and hours of labour went by without any knowledge of toil.

I knew that one day I would have to live on the mountain; and highly personal as that might seem, it was not subjectively so. The topmost house on Slieve Gullion was not more than three miles from the centre of the parish at the church in Dromintee; yet people in the fields and bogs resented the outsiders who classified them as 'Mountainees'. Inside the parish, the Mountainees were held to be a backward, clannish, secretive people who kept together in assemblies outside and inside the church at Mass, at fair or dance. The Mountainees themselves, instinctively aware of social levels and divisions, showed acute sensitivities of their own. They suspected satire where none was intended; they observed a deeper sense of communal attachment, were more traditional, more conservative, and spoke with aggressive pride of house and hillock and clutch of erratic, high-ditched fields won by forebears from the whin and boulder, the bracken and heather.

I would be a stranger to such a people, but never to the spirit of the mountain itself.

I did not live on the mountain until I had married, when my wife and I went into Ketty Buck's cabin on Garriba up the Slieve Gullion mountain road. Necessity more than choice had brought fulfilment to the wish; but its spiritual hunger still lived.

Only people from the towns refer to one-storey country houses as cottages, and earn the secret annoyance and resentment of the owner: only such people, and local satirists, would call my house a cabin. The term in South Armagh vernacular was 'a house of one bay'. It is of primitively simple structure. A wooden partition separates room from kitchen. In the room there is place for a bed, a chair and stool and a small chest of drawers; it has a small window and an open grate. In the kitchen, if I stand at one wall and hold a sweeping brush at arms' length, I can touch 'the back of the house'. The house has a slated roof, and if I raise the brush to the naked rafters I can touch the ridge board. An open fireplace and whitewashed walls, a low door, two upright gables, and that is the cabin. Spring water can be drawn from a well under a huge boulder in the yard, or 'street', just midway between the door and the gate. Birds bathe of mornings in the rushy outlet of the well and some nights the frogs croak.

The cabin, like all the houses up that road, lies under the shelter of the long ridge of Garriba. Garriba is a perfect glacial tail tapering southwards like a limb out of Slieve Gullion, with the heath and heather giving way to irregular little fields bound by seams of tall, stone ditches.

The ridge rises further on and links up with the hill in the south where the twin rocks of the Dhaaicklemore jut buck teeth at the sky. Midway stands St Patrick's Catholic church – from the kitchen window through whins on the ditch I can see the belfry, which made a crib for a Christmas Star for me – looking as grey as if hewn from a rock when this world was born. Past my gate the mountain road begins to ascend in a long nervous wriggle. On the right of it, the great wilderness of Slieve Gullion; on the left, as if in the lap of the recumbent mountain, the erratic run of fields, with green arms around the throats of rocks, studded with houses, some white with life, others as grey in death as old ditches.

From my door I look out on hills over small fields and bogs. To the south the Dhaaicklemore ends in three leaps of rock to a cleft which makes the echoing Glen Dhu. Ending in a seashell twist near the same glen, at right angles to the other hill, the Bohil Breaga has summit-hacked pedestals where the evening sun blazes in wonderful beams... or where the mist-scrolls before west rain squeeze slowly, like cotton wool deadening the sounds in an ear. West beyond Monribba Bog and the Black Road to Longfield, the village of Forkhill on rising terraces of land, like a tired wing-spread bird, shows against a fall of rock quarried by time from the slope of Crosslieve – Creshla to the people.

Inside the cabin, and starting at the fire – always the centre of social life in the Irish countryside – we have the open grate and a hob on either side, with a chain hanging from a bar across the chimney high up: no crane or crooks. There is no settlebed nor a half door. I do not mind the settlebed, but I do miss the half door.

It keeps out its quota of draughts, could be lifted off to provide a dancing-deck for nimble feet at a ceilidh; but better than all, when you leaned over it of an evening with a pipe going you were half in the house, half outside at the same time; you could keep in touch with people and conversation inside and, if necessary, outside as well. Here I could make my ceilidh with the birds, or the sights and sounds from the Monribba Bog road, and it afforded a pleasant excuse for passing time.

I wish there had been a half door to my cabin, for as well as everything else it would have provided one with the habit of pause and thus auto-suggested one to stoop, so that I would have saved my head (and the heads of some visitors) a few over-smart rappings against the top of the door-cheek.

It took me a month to acquire and obey the instinct to duck; and even so, when hurrying out I may rise the head too soon:

after a stumble one ends up sometimes on one's knees in the street, and not in prayer either.

'The house is low so the door must be low': thus reasoned many of the Irish builders. Porches had not become fashionable; you walked over the threshold right into the kitchen. They aimed at snugness and an escape from winds, so doors were low too. Many doors were in fact built to suit the physique of the original owner, and much the same principle seems to have determined the making of doorways in outhouses for cattle and pigs. They had, of course, to think always of expense and economy.

People tell me however: 'Well, it's lonely and a bit inconvenient, but it's a compact wee place, and easy kept clean.'

I am not sure, and Alice, my wife, is certain it is not. Garriba ridge shields us from the east wind, but if it does, it creates a whirlblast ('furl-blast' is our idiom) from the tumble and rebound of other winds and the drop of the hill; and then the wee cabin smokes like a forge.

The cabin has an individuality of its own, and as many a good horse has its kick, perhaps the wee house must have its smoke. The trick of wedging a bottomless bucket in the chimney made no improvement, nor did a board that could flap in the wind help either. The revolving pot or a modern gadget is no doubt a proper remedy, but that would hurt the dignity of the cabin and all it stands for in this environment.

This environment, like the social facilities of a half door in a lesser sense, enables the mood of the house to stand half within the mystic spirit of Slieve Gullion, while yet in touch with ordinary life below. It has lowland peace touched with the solitude of the mountain, and even appears to be able to draw some meaning from the personality of the bog. All the affinities that must always exist between man and field and crop and nature seem to find a touchstone in the mood of the cabin.

There is time to reflect with a fresh insight. Slieve Gullion may be a temple, I a solitary worshipper, but I find myself taking an interest deeper than ever in local topics. It used always puzzle us in the valleys to hear how folk on the mountain knew all the goings-on of the parish much sooner than ourselves.

This is largely, if not fundamentally, due to the physical sense of isolation. From the mountain one's social range lies spread before one's eyes, as intimate as the familiar humps and hollows in an earthen floor. Two smokes in a house (someone ill in the room?), a knot of people on a road, an incident breaking the rhythm of work in a field – any glance can reveal all this and more. Curiosity is inevitable. For you also realise that, no matter how subtly the social levels may exist, one is part of the deeper throb of the parochial community. This awareness gives an astonishing life to thought; and you understand why the people below think the mountainy folk cute and cunning, instead of noting how they've sharpened their wits on stoic perception. You understand why they economise in speech, and why they must sometimes be sardonic. But then Slieve Gullion can appear to be sardonic as well. For every speculation comes back for reference to the mountain.

I feel oddly disturbed when away from the mountain; as if my absence were betraying the spirit which is apt to impart in a final mood the message that would round off in true satisfaction this urge to get inside so that my own spirit might settle in peace.

For the mountain can communicate. Maud Gonne wrote to me that Slieve Gullion had sung to her so clearly that she could write down the air. It spoke to me as if its changing moods wrote cryptic messages on the inside of the mind and heart. I found that voice re-echoing the speech of human reality in all and every hill and house, in field and fair, wake and wedding, and the events of people at home and abroad: I wanted to interpret it in terms of common clay.

It speaks with another reality too. Here on Garriba, for instance, is a field almost ready for the seed. The earth has been reclaimed from whin and bracken after almost one hundred years of abandonment: not even the oldest man on our mountain road remembers that field having been laboured. The reality lies in the vision of watching time retrace to relive an earlier moment of history. For this feat of labour is the kind of triumph which people had to attain when they first trekked into these hills three hundred years ago, driven from the level acres in the planted north. And the field becomes part of the living voice of the mountain solitude that is never silent, and we all share in it.

The image of men and women and children stripping heather like hair from the stubborn breast of our mountainsides, to expose the dark, peaty flesh of the soil to the kiss of light and the seed of life, has always moved and stirred me. But never so movingly as now when I live in a mountain cabin of one bay on Slieve Gullion itself.

BOG ROAD GOSSIP ON A WINTRY DAY

It was no day to be breasting the weather on our bog road, even though it always has an individuality, and at times the fragile atmosphere of fairy paths. But not on a day like this. Every hilltop wore a cloud like a cocked hat encrusted with snow, with a grey cloak of drizzling sky behind. Now and then a gust tore up as if determined to clear a way for the trailing curtains of rain and tried to throttle a lone bush. And it swept the bog road as it would a winter promenade.

Leaving the surface torrents and clabber of our mountain road, the bog road ran wide before me. Instantly, my eye fastened on a figure ahead, coming towards me from the far hill. He wore a loose 'swinger' of a coat, too, for its tails flapped plainly as a blast birled him halfways across the road from the poor shelter of the hedges.

The bog itself was like a sea, and mirrored all the shivering bleakness of the winter's day as the rain tweaked at it. Between the gusts, one heard the headlong rush of the river from Slieve Gullion, gargled by the rocky throat on the glen above Clough-innea. Not a bird stirred from the bushes. Not a beast could be seen in the fields. Beyond the bog someone had started a first ploughing of stubbles. The door of every house was shut and glistening dully, and when smoke twitched from a chimney it was booted by the wind.

And then he came up, half-crouched. I had long since identified him by his walk; I would recognise that footstep on the darkest night. The overcoat reached well below his shins, and his hat, like my own, had seen better days and kinder weather.

'There's weather for yeh, if yeh like!' he shouted, stripping his teeth in a *cár* as he wheeled on to one foot like something at anchor, or the end of its tether, to squint and blubber into the

9

rain. We stood shoulder to shoulder, our heads tipped side-ways. To the gods of the elements, high, dry and sardonic on their roosts above the weather of the world, we might have resembled two dilapidated jackdaws, ousted from their chimney nest and trying to reconcile themselves to their misery.

'It'll kill the country – this weather!' he shouted.

'It's past talkin' about!' I shouted back.

'What did yeh say?' And his head came round, sideways. The gust flipped speech as it left your mouth.

'It's a holy divine terror!' I said.

'Aw now – it's past talkin' about…'

Now we could hear the roar of the mountain river again; and even hear the gust, on its way east, cascade through the trees in the graveyard at Dromintee on the tail of the ridge above us. Then a blackbird stirred and flew across the road, as if on a fledgling's wings.

'It's been an awful time for rain – aye, an' everythin'… God save us, but the people all had a deal o' trouble lately. Ah well… sure that's the way. A body never knows what's afore them, an' sure it's just as well that way – no, an' dammit, but a helluva sight better…' And he smacked his lips and opened his mouth as if gasping. I was watching a bit of straw now, where it rocked on a puddle, as if it might reveal its significance in the scheme of the universe. But suddenly he whipped his hand from his overcoat pocket and showed a portion of butter on his wide, crusty palm.

'Lookit what's to do a man for a week… Yeh wouldn't need to get wicked at that to gollop it at one feed. It's shockin' times,' he said, putting the ration back, and turning till we were again shoulder to shoulder. 'An' the lard, God bless me – an' they wrap it if yeh don't mind. Many a time I left more grease in the wrinkles o' me boots. It's shockin' times sure enough.'

I made to move on, when he said again: 'Oul Peadar on our road's bad.'

'Since when?'

'Ah… he can't be the thing this while: there's two smokes in the house this week an' more. He had the priest an' doctor. Coorse' – with a step forward, a shrug and a shuffling back; he doesn't want to be the author of a rumour – 'there's no sign of death on him; but sure what am I talking about? Sure that says nothin' in these times. Still… the years is there…'

'Aye… the years is there.'

'Aye, an' there's no tellin' at all when a man gets up in years an' him ailin'…' Now he palmed his growth of beard as if puzzled to find it there. 'Well, as they used to say, "The want o' the people is a poor want." An' Kate's away to Yankee land…'

I was watching a field where the heaps of top-dressing lay half spread, musing maybe on spring, and didn't pick up his phrase – even though he said it with the customary inflection of half-query, the precaution of the news-vendor.

'Kate… Kate… Aw, no?'

'Aye, boy.' His shoulders gave a heave. 'Put out the fire for the first an' last time an' turned the key in the oul' thatch cabin. Off be air to Yankee land. It was lonely be herself.' He wasn't being sentimental: it was one of the few surviving thatched houses. One thought of a night when music and dance welcomed the emigrants there…

'I say… Didn't we mark the time an' place to meet for a crack. As raw a day as ever I mind. But I think she has a notion to take up…'

And he went his way. When I returned to that spot, someone was spreading the heaps of top-dressing. The river roared continually. Far off, a colour yellow as lamplight touched the gauzy draperies of the rain; then a chink in the west blazed out, like a spot-hole in a furnace door. It fell eerily on the flooded bog and clung to the houses. Somewhere, a thrush sang in the murky haze of strange light, as if among this winter snore of rain and wind and wet lyrical light it had caught a sign of the first stirring of spring.

SPIRIT OF A SPRING MORNING

The mind's eye sees it and the instinct senses it, quick as thought: a new presence which was not around the morning before, nor the day before, nor the night before.

A subtle quickening of a gay urgency which seems at any moment as if about to transfigure the dour bog, the bent, grey stone ditches over the skyline of Garriba, the air of loneliness on the morning road.

Yesterday evening a peach sky with a star in its throat silhouetted a ploughman at Slieve Gullion's foot into mystical allegory – yet it was not around. But of its presence this morning there is no doubt. And catching its breath, you stop, even though on the way to a morning weekday Mass.

There had been rain during the night, but it did no more than kiss the stones and darken the soil of the ploughed fields. It did not even extinguish the fire smouldering for almost a week in the bog; for it still smoked in a blue skein as delicate as the faded willow pattern on an aged and dusty plate on top of a dresser in some ancient thatched house.

Here and there, however, a living house doffed a plume of smoke to this new spirit of morning. But the pastures as yet were empty and the other fields still. Upended ploughs and spring-harrows, with sole-plates polished by wear, lay on headlands or against the briars to one side of a gap. And every gap lay open, the earth around it pitted with tracks.

A bird pecked a straw from a field dunghill and flew away. On a chimney nearby the jackdaws were already rowdy, building a nest. A red lorry came down John Bwee's Hill near Myles's. In Famine relief the hill had been cut into steep ditches of stone and earth, and the lorry might have been a ball trundling down an alley. Silently it slid from the hill along the level road through Flurry's Bog without any visible bump till it glided over the high-backed bridge; but as it charged for the hill I heard its engine scream.

Over the hill by the chapel it went with a final burst and roar towards Forkhill... and then there was a lark somewhere. A thrush, too, in the bent, gnarled trees of the graveyard. A goat grazing on a high ditch whipped up its head as I came abreast – and then I saw the kid tucked behind a whin.

Now that I had a broadside view of the smoke from the bog fire it seemed to have vanished; no more than a hint of vapoury blue, still as a painting. Silently, too, and steaming north, a train deep in the cutting of Faughil unravelled a steam-and-smoke thread of grey expanding wool behind it. Then a little herd of cattle appeared on John Bwee's Hill, and, though the driver was an indistinct though smart-stepping speck, I recognised the man as Jemmy Ned.

Someone turned the corner of the chapel swiftly and hurried through the open half of the main door. Down the road a cyclist was pedalling. Among other cycles along the chapel wall was one with two milking-cans hanging from the handlebars. And the thrush in the gnarled trees, that look like collogueing old men, was singing its heart out as if trying to rouse them.

In the chapel porch the boots of weekday wear embarrassed one by their clanging on the tiles. How an echo can chastise in church... Inside, a small bird was flying from window to window, resting, flying again, and once it perched on the high altar. Some youngsters watched it: so did I. Isn't spring a prayer too?... Faith, hope and charity emanating from God's good earth?... With the austerity of winter to purify the evils of clay by frost pangs and bitter winds in preparation for the wholesome uplifting of life in the glory and resurrection of Easter.

Thus did I pardon distraction during Mass.

The side door of the chapel was open also and someone flitted by. Then came a sudden burst of cawing from crows. I remembered a Sunday here in Dromintee during Mass when a

14

hare had sped by that door, pursued by a dog – and both pursued by the excited, earthy encouragement of the hunter – with nigh-profane objurgation too when the dog couldn't turn the hare... and, as we said, 'the chapel smiled'.

Someone came in behind me, knelt down and banished distraction for another moment. For then the altar bell rang at the Sanctus (it is really a gong) and its echo tapered away in the silence... tapered away... luring imagination to the great symbolical echo of Life and God... and the Irish spring. When I had rung that bell myself as an altarboy, that same tapering sound had always fascinated me into distraction... and, for some reason I could never fathom then, I kept thinking always of the exiles...

Next moment one reproves oneself for renewed distraction, and a moment later watches a woman wriggle her head free from a dark grey shawl and immediately begin to cowl it up again!

Boots crunch on the shingle in the chapel yard, pound through the doorway, pause at the holy water font, and then clatter uninhibitedly up the aisle: a schoolboy, overcoat lumped under one arm, shapeless schoolbag under the other, broken strap dangling.

Mass continues...

Along the road outside a cart with iron-shod wheels jolts past, unmistakeably loaded with harrows. On the long rein behind and treading the cart's thunder, comes the echoing clop of the other horse of the team.

There was a moment of living silence which wrapped the intonations of Latin from the altar with awe, touching prayer with mystery and a new fervency; while the feminine trill of a robin, perched on a tombstone, trickled in through the side door which held the dome of Slieve Gullion as a backcloth.

Now children were running past the chapel on the road. Some of them paused, gabbling. A girl's voice came through distinctly:

'Well, amn't I silly! I said a prayer to St Anthony to find me me pen an' pencil, an' they're not in me bag at all.' She ran off, still talking, bound for school. Somewhere a cow was bawling and a dog barked. A human voice said something indistinct faraway.

Mass was over.

Outside, the few men among the congregation (friends and neighbours of the soul for whom the Mass had been offered) halted habitually on the roadside in a group and lit pipes. I joined them. A boy raced past us shouting to his companions ahead: 'Our goat's kidded... Seamus... Our goat's kidded in Anne Corny's whins.'

We mightn't have existed.

The bog fire was smoking again, visibly. In the fields men were yoking teams to ploughs and harrows. On one hillside of ploughed land a flock of gulls looked like the remains of a passing shower of hail, and two boys chased them into a gusty feather-flight by flinging clods of earth.

A woman was saying as she came through the chapel gate: '...she's no way smart at the sums, but she can fair ate the Catechism, an' sure that's a good thing an' Confirmation so close...'

The sky had been heavy enough when I had gone to Mass; but now the sun was coming through over Slieve-na-Bola, and it made brassy rods in the stairs of cloud. The rods seemed to fill and sag, swinging to earth, to rock and field, breaking on the high-flung houses of the Hip of Carnagore and the surrounds of dead bracken.

It broke, too, on Glen Dhu and Balnamadda; and the sight was somehow like the sensation of the cry of blood to blood in an awareness of kinship and renewed greeting. At such a moment of spring's awakening I know again that these townlands have wrought their mould, past and present, into my character. Not even the isolated rocks are inarticulate just then.

An eight-bull harrow with iron pins was combing the scutchy skull of a field, chuckling among the clay and stones. Further along, schoolboys stood at a gap appealing to a ploughman.

16

'A what?' came the ploughman's laughing cry. 'You want me to let you have a scrape?' As if from deep in an earthy throat, he reproved them with more sober laughter: 'Away you to your school, boy; an' if you have any grace or luck in life you'll never know what it is to take the handles of a plough in your hands... A scrape?... Dick, pony – hop aff... Kate, girl – go down... G'down I tell yous – Ah, Dick, man – Kate – go down... G'down.'

WOMEN IN THE FIELDS AT SPRING

As a twin in a pair of realistic symbols – the earthy reek of burning scutch is the other – I remember women, and women I worked for in our little fields at spring.

Remembering the women in the fields is enough to induce me, on a spirit of seasonal wellbeing, to toss to the forgiving magic of the spring breezes the ideas and conflicting notions which different people feel from the sight, sound and utterance of the word 'peasant'.

None of my people, or those I worked for, ever used the word – as a Frenchman or Belgian, say, will use it quite naturally. Many I worked and lived among had never heard it except from a book, some never understood what it meant. So that we use it in literature only, and then as a label, often mawkishly, often without title or right.

Nevertheless it still remains, like harvest, a holy expression, something more than a word or mere name; an expression of wonder, of dignity, of a life and living in terms good and bad, with a feeling of pattern and a human rhythm arising purely from a colourful and poetic sound: a symbol of a word.

And everyone who is wise in spring trades in some magic of mind, man and woman, that touches on symbols. But almost everyone is wise in spring. And this woman is one of my symbols.

How does she appear?

Maybe as she persists in appearing to me: in a small shawl or handkerchief-cowl tied below the chin, or if long enough, knotted simply high on her breast. She wears long skirts and a 'bag apron' of sacking, which she calls a *bráiscín* in Gaelic. Ankle-length boots, or cast-offs from the men, are often laced with cord; the clay of the fields and the potato drills would, as

19

she says, 'only destroy half-decent boots' and twist and turn them out of shape. And then there is the dung to soil and stain them as well.

That is one image. There is another – if you would swop the skirts for corduroys or dungarees, drape her town-packed waves with a 'colleen' headscarf, and set her astride a tractor seat with a cigarette in lips as vivid and red as wild poppy in early oats. Both images are still twins; both are still symbols of the realistic evolution of woman in the spring fields.

The older image must seem to conflict with the later. We remember the older one expressing disgust and disgrace on her sex when the younger appeared – first of all – with her cigarette. But don't we remember the old woman in the fields who kept her short clay pipe tucked within her breast apparel, or somewhere within a secret recess of voluminous skirts – and the flash of red flannel as she wrought and sought to find it: *lips* red with you, miss; *petticoat* with the other.

...Remember, after all, our grandmothers smoking short clays, praying blessings in Gaelic on the fields and the working women they could no longer join; sitting in groups on a green ditch, talking in Gaelic, smoking the clays and consuming little more than a good pipeful in a week – but all of it ounce-plug or 'hard chaw', as we said: one back whiff of it enough, admittedly, to take the breath off the young of either sex in splutter and cough and cast of a baleful eye.

On or off the tractor – in or out of the fields for good – she is still the woman who wielded her graip of four steel prongs to spread dung in the drills; who bent once at every yard of the same drill to drop (our vernacular for planting) seed potatoes from that 'bag *bráiscín*' tied about her waist and weighted, according to the length of the drill, with maybe three stone each time.

She was the woman who came to the headrig with 'dinner for the field' and after the meal – amid compliments satirical and genuine, the teasing and the earthy, adult repartee in traditional phrases about love and marriage and children or the lack of them – she stayed to help. Sometimes she owned the field, sometimes she was there as a neighbour to 'give a hand', unbidden except by the edict of communal instinct, and sometimes, like myself, she was working for wages.

Gnarl-minded old labourers used advise us: 'Never work for a woman. A woman never knows what's in a day's work.'

It often seemed to be true… till you remembered her in early spring, with pigs, calves and cattle and new broods of swarming chickens around her feet on top of her housework; as well as secret settings of 'oul' clockin' hens' – lest himself become aware of the rising hosts of brooders and raise holy murder over a conception of chickens of all breeds and ages rooting in new corn in the Hungry Month of June, when no food, or 'meat' as he'd say, seemed to fill any kind of bird or beast.

In between the preparation and the hectic scamper of setting and sowing, she found time to 'cut the seed'. You could find her kitchen quiet and empty, except, perhaps, for an early brood snuggling on a sack on the corner of the floor under the hen, the dust of the remains of the oatmeal food and droppings on the sack. She was nowhere to be seen. Usually you came upon her finding 'idle time' to get to a barn or open shed or carthouse, where she squatted on a creepie stool, or perhaps on her knees, bent over a heap of potatoes which she was slitting expertly to 'make seed' which has just enough 'eyes', or buds, and no more (or you gouged these out) and so make ordinary whole potatoes go further in the economy of the setting.

Or sometimes you found her giving a hand to an old woman who had come to do the task for wages. When we saw these waifs, most of them 'going the roads' in spring, their dark shawls about them, we knew they were off to cut seed for someone; glad to get the money, for many of them subsisted on 'relief' doled out in the local dispensary each week.

You remember both of them in the open shed – letting light and the harsh airs of March dry the cut potatoes to 'put a skin on the seed'; their eyes tired and strained, their limbs stiff and cold, cutting each potato into the heart of their hands, with skill and knowledge swiftly guiding the blade, yet all so

21

casually done.

Always it was the women who dropped seed.

'They have the back for it,' the men said – sometimes wryly, even evasively; but it was a belief then. When a man had his potato drills ready for planting he used say jocosely, but half-wishfully: 'Man, if only two or three tight, strappin' lumps o' weeman would slip a *bráiscín* about them an' drop me me seed, I'd have the field in in jink time.'

You remember her at the job, her fingers all 'false nails'; the skin and cuticle at the nail-ends slit and curled back and pained and often bled from quick contact of placing each cut seed firmly in the dry manure of stable, byre and pigsty. Some of them made reputations:

'She touched every seed with us the day.'

She didn't, like us, merely bend over and drop the seed from a height – if we were let.

She taught our infant fingers to drop seed potatoes in the first place, and always in the garden. With one of her old boots tied on top of our own feet, she showed us how to gauge the distance between each seed by making you put a heel before a seed and a seed beyond a toe; lift your double-booted foot, then heel-and-toe again. You learned – and longed – to get on with the task without the weight of a maternal boot: for we all went barefoot then coming on to spring.

She could, for all that, be a bit of a tyrant; for she was still a peasant; and the peasant complex could put the demands of house, fields, cattle or crops above the rightful need and call of people, even her own. She had prides too, and simple human joys in communal activities.

On the day she came to the headrig of a spring field with tea in a four or eight-quart can, a basket on her arm, maybe one in the other hand, and a white cloth tossed across her shoulder, she was proud. (There was a time and place for the day when, along with another woman, she came with a small tub of champ of mashed potatoes swinging in a bed sheet, with rolls of butter in cans of buttermilk to be knifed into plates of champ to make a golden dip.)

22

She was proud and showed it in the glow on her face because of the sight of so many workers – even though she had made allowances with extra mugs for those who had come unbidden by word or hint. This 'sight of people' was a reflection and a measure of her esteem among the neighbours.

'Hoigh – Hoigh! Drop what's yous're at an' come on. Empty your *bráiscín*s...'

Some feigned to linger over a job and she called again, admonishingly. The women in the field came slowly to the headrig, and like everyone else, pounded down the briars with their twisted boots before sinking or dropping to rest, and making jocose exclamations that tried to conceal the cry of real weariness.

Traditional phrase was on hand with ready-made excuses:
'The big fall hard...' With a laugh.
'Aye... Down, however I'll get up...'
'Ah – they're low that God can't rise...'

On her knees the woman herself is handing out mugs of tea; others pass them along the row of workers sitting and squatting against the ditch. The split farls of soda bread squelching butter are also passed along. Eggs and spoons – maybe tossed to someone – with grains of salt in twists of paper, each to serve three or four.

And if sufficient drinking mugs still aren't on hand, himself will charitably 'wait on a mug' until someone has eaten, while another may drink out of the lid of a can. The dog awaits the scraps to be thrown, for fingers haven't been washed, and anyhow tradition says you should throw away the last bite, lest Hungry Grass grow around the site of such a scrapless meal.

Chat and talk and banter move in light and allusive shade – sometimes garbed in the words of traditional euphemisms if the knowing young are present, though jokes at their expense, which as yet they don't understand, bring wild laughter from the older ones. ('Ah, me pipe, *a mhic*... Thank yeh... Good man... That the hair may grow in *thamog*s where it never grew afore.') In light and shade the talk flows almost in time to the

23

cloud shadows, with the banter and wit swirling in free and adult companionship like the spill of notes from excited blackbirds swooping over the ditch.

Such is the woman as I remember her: always valiant, rarely complaining; often the backbone and brains of man and the land, guardian and guide of the tillage fields; possessive, maybe, but with human aches paining somewhere in each pride. One always remembers the whys and wherefores – she was the main victim in the end of every whim of history at all levels, even on her own floor among the customs of her clan.

Yet who could keep the new bride out of the spring fields of her new homestead?

Not even a government decree.

'Let yous rest yourselves now… Rest can't yous… Yous are slaughterin' yourselves,' she said when the meal in the field was over, though she knew she had to be as anxious as any to see the work completed.

You remember the tale of the woman from tradition: 'You can rest yourself after your dinner diggin' the garden for me…'

'Never work for a woman: she doesn't know what's in a day's work…'

Maybe the soured old men were right: she often did not know; she was too used to the task of having to put two and three days' work into one herself. Beauty never boiled the pot – nor grumbling either – nor for that matter, turned a sod of earth or dropped a seed priddy.

SUMMER EVENING AT SLIEVE GULLION

Where we sat, a railing had one time enclosed a rostrum of green and a few trees before the door of the house. The green and the trees survive, although two of them show traces of scorch; for the house is one of our relics of what we still call the 'Trouble'. Long since, the railing had been removed from the low wall, and where turrets of coping remained we had taken seats, oddly distributed sure enough. Summer is surely here when the men gather at McGuill's; and it seemed the natural thing to sit where a ledge of coping remained.

The house had been wonderfully situated, commanding a powerful view. The birds still sing in the overhead branches; and when you turn to look up you see the spires of the church belfry piercing the firs on the hill to your left, and its greys a mild pink in the evening light. We sat with our backs to the house to face the valley, the bog, the maze of hedges lush with new leaf, the hills beyond and Slieve Gullion at our shoulder.

Naturally enough, the men were recalling incidents from the life which once radiated around the ruined house behind us; of characters and rollicking episodes, of a toleration of impulse and ready spirit which they lamented as gone for ever... Maybe ironed out by the new self-consciousness, or just waiting the proper mood to strike off again. Now and then someone rose from his coping perch to stride into the road and make a gesture, to demonstrate or mimic some act or person figuring in his story and then back he came to the remains of the wall to sit and look into the west towards the village. Their caps were tilted till the peaks almost touched the tip of the nose.

No one had seen the country and the crops looking so well for their time in the ground. Maybe it was contrast and the abrupt burst of buds that made one see a richer-than-ever tone in colour. There was even a strange intensity about the emerald depth and purity of new growth on the bog; it made old rushes look red, while the thickets of bog sallies spun an airy purple over their delicate greens from something as grey as lichen. The first flush of green was among the heather too, and every house might have been freshly whitewashed, the way west walls and gables soaked the light. And in the garden of the ruined house – across the road before us – a crab-apple tree, like a child's hair ribbons, sported a garland of blossom.

Two youths joined us and lay on their backs full length on the green, rising to their elbows only when a car came down the hill and droned at speed over the bog road. Each time, they debated its make and year, while the men surmised who the driver might be. And then the dreaminess settled back on speech as they looked longsomely into the west across the apple tree.

Suddenly, over a remark of mine, one of the men went into the road and, with his stick, pointed out on the dead walls where the ornamental deers' heads used to be placed in summers long ago. I watched him as he leaned on his stick... as his eyes went over what remained of the walls, before he returned and sat down. Not really insensible to the note that quickens emotion, a word or two is as much as the countryman can utter in appreciation without sentiment becoming uneasy.

And then, pointing to the bog, he recalled a harvest when he carted corn from there with a blood horse. I could scarcely believe him. But others pointed to rushy land beyond, even naming fields lost to whin on the hills; of houses gone and ceilidhers going to and fro in the darkness with bits of lighted turf for torches. It was the kind of talk that, bit by bit, was plaiting a mood to net the butterfly spirit of another era; plaiting the reality of an old charm with a fantasy that saw, in the very arrangement of the hills, symbols of the dream life of the people, and an insight to their own mysticism... Temples that might house the slumbering gods...

Just then, behind a mass of little clouds like a stretched woollen garment, the light was going. I watched the hilltops.

The Bohil Breaga of Tiffcrum, with shade behind each fold, tapered like a seashell towards Glen Dhu – the half door to Slieve Gullion, with one cottage framed wistfully in the gap. Creshla Mountain, twin-peaked above Forkhill – loveliest village of the North – flipped enough sunlight to catch the topmost branches of the trees and glorify their shades of first leaf above the blush of fresh earth. Here a surge of land seems to rise against the cascade of stone and heather; but there is a magic glen between, watched by a tower at a lake, where cabins perch on spouts of rocky land as a Disney lightship might sit on the crest of a wave.

A girl went by from milking her cows, the milk throbbing on the bottom of her cans with a sound like the far away beating of drums. 'God bless the work,' someone said, but she was a young girl and we no more than heard her 'Thank yeh'. A flying night beetle zoomed towards the apple tree. And a man coming straight from his fields brought the exciting presence of that awesome strength of character which clings mystically to the countryman in the shadows.

Dusk was on Cloughinnea now, most mystical place of the valley. On one of its rocks a fairy thorn rose as if to beat the embers of a burnt-out skyline dropping behind it. Here the crimson knots of cloud were turning purple; while further on, nearer Slieve Gullion, a roof and its chimney, in bronze-edged silhouette, dribbled smoke against a brandy sky. A faint whisper of petal perfume sweetened the air; and as we rose to go, each corncrake sounded like the other's echo.

THE OLD MAN AND THE TINKERS

I was coming down one side of the nill and they down the other, while the evening sun in early summer madness blazed across Garriba.

I didn't notice his flitting at first, because the pony and cart had got caught in a tinker camp moving from the direction of the border.

But in the hollow, where runs the sweetest and now the only roadside water between the town of Newry and our end of Slieve Gullion, the leading tinker van pulled in. The boy in charge of his flitting tried to pull out of the convoy, but the pony chucked back.

Then I heard the ould fella. 'It must be good water,' he was saying apologetically, divertingly, too. 'No beast ever cares to pass it, I notice.' And then I saw him, one hand resting on the characteristic furniture on the wee cart, while with the other he wiped his face with the inside of his cap.

All the time a host of vicious, quizzical and dour-looking tinkers of all ages and sexes and degrees of cleanliness gawked in a resentful silence over front splay-boards and through overhanging hair; through collections of hooped hazel rods, a goat's horns and mounds of sacking topped with death haw-thorns plundered, no doubt, from a wayside gap or hedge.

The boy saw there was nothing for it but wait his turn at the drinking place, though his warm face took on the deeper flush of embarrassment. The ould fella noticed it and chuckled as he crossed to the mossy ditch where he nudged a briar aside before sitting down, face to the sun. I sat beside him and, habitually, we both tilted our caps over our noses to make eyeshades.

'That's a wicked, weakenin' heat,' he said and cleared his

31

throat lustily. Then he plucked a *cuiseog* of grass and put it between his teeth while he surveyed his flitting on the pony cart.

'God pardon me,' he went on ruefully, yet with a wry humour, 'but you'd never believe a body had such a gether-up of ould junk an' thrumpery till you come to shift it.'

Just then the tinker van pulled out from the water and he added perplexedly but amusingly: 'An' when all's said an' done... they have the right end of the story. Would that be the tinker sold me the leakin' can?... An' I kept sour milk in it for a week, too. They get away with near-murder where you an' me would swing for a lot less.'

But his laugh was shaky just the same. I asked him why he was leaving his house.

He didn't reply at once. 'Sure I had too...' And from the back of his head he tipped his cap further over his eyes.

'...For why?'

'Kippered – that's why. Pure bleddywell kippered with the smoke.' He added quickly: 'This is gettin' to be a woeful country. They send out inspectors to see that a cow beast has a clean house to lie in; but barrin' you have the itch or the yalla jack or worse, curse the one puts a nose near the Christian barrin' he's half dead. A woeful country sure enough.'

Another tinker van pulled away, but there was still another before his flitting could draw in. The tinkers didn't speak, not even among themselves; nor did the menfolk and the older women as much as glance at us as they drove away in turn. Even their white terrier, with a scald-scar on its side, snubbed our society and didn't give a look, let alone a growl.

When I looked at the ould fella again he was staring back towards his old home. A shade was creeping like ink over a blotter across house and field, ditch and bog, edging towards Carnagore and Slieve-na-Bola, where ploughed lands, bent and curved by the hillside, were as red as the rusted board of a swing plough half hidden in the rising green of fresh grasses.

Suddenly a goat kid blahhed as if knifed, and looking towards the hilltop before us, a boy, in silhouette against the sunset, was chasing a goat; the goat turned and reared and butted, and using his coat like a bull-fighter's cloak I watched him tease the animal, intrigued with the fantasy of the dream outline. Someone was shouting that calves had broken into the hay. And all the time the ould fella was staring at his old home.

Magic had touched it. The sun had bronzed part of the roof, and the fairy thorn growing before the door had caught a secret reflection to show off in new beauty the perfectly round growth of its foliage. But how lonely it looked without someone to admire it from over a half door. As I watched I'm sure a lone breeze preened its leaves...

And the ould fella was saying: 'It's an ancient ould place, anyway... an' always was...' Another tinker van moved off, but he didn't give it a glance. 'I mind to see that house one night with every window blazin' the way the chapel windows are blazin' now, an' the place crammed with straw. An' not a slate or stone turned or harmed the next mornin'. Thon ould bushes are there since the year o' one, an' the stones are like ould faces.'

The boy pulled out with his flitting. 'You've no call,' he began timidly, as if he had long since rehearsed his speech, 'to be puttin' another journey on yourself. I'll manage this load off meself. Have that last load of thrumpery ready when I get back.'

'May God increase you, *a mhic*,' sighed the ould fella. 'To tell the truth, me feet have me crucified in this heat.' The boy went on and we sat where we were. 'A flittin',' mused the ould fella, 'leaves me as tired as an ould horse.'

I knew it did. Not so much due to the physical toil as to spiritual uprootment, which absorbs nervous energy like secret drinking; uprootment from walls and corners and places which have become grazing lands for personality.

And the ould fella mused on. The last of the tinkers had long since gone when he told of other flittings and evictions he remembered when the landlords ruled the roost. 'Not, mind you,' he shot in, 'but if some of us had their chance we could expect anythin' better. Still –' he winked secretly and made a grimace, 'God be to wink betimes when the tip of luck misses one beggar to make another a king. Luck's a king, an' luck's a beggar...'

We were still sitting when the boy appeared on the hill of the road above us. The ould fella bounded up at once, but groaned as his feet hit the hard road. Shade had wand-power now, making the hills unreal and airy, the ditches a maze that led thought to fairyland and mystery. In the dimming lights I watched him hurry-hobble for his last load of thrumpery from 'the ancient ould place', while the hills toasted rocky shins at the hearthstone of evening as old men brood over the embers of their memories.

HOLIDAY FOR RURAL IRELAND

Gala day – the fifteenth of August! – Rural Ireland's one and only holiday at once religious and civil, national and traditional.

Man, woman and child used to head for the sea on this day, and many still do.

I remember a time when, before a body would stay around their own door on this day, they would need to be crippled, dead, or dying, the cow about to calve – or yourself maybe penniless.

But for a few weeks beforehand the hens could stop laying, according to the old people; maybe disappear altogether into a fowl-man's crate, their going blamed on the fox. Thus did some from our country manage, on the fifteenth, to see the Point or the Rocks, abbreviations still used for Warrenpoint in Co. Down, and Blackrock in Co. Louth.

Even when we were too young to go, we stowed away on the brakes and, when discovered, were chucked off. It was good to watch the people assemble, for it was novelty. Only the wise men carried coats and had to endure much jibing for their wisdom. A few had melodeons. Ah... the wonderful world that lay beyond the hilltops dreaming in the Point or the Rocks...

For how many times did we see them return in the open brake, wet to the skin; new clothes creased like a bag you've sat upon and a melodeon in 'champ'. Still, everyone made jokes about the wet. Aye... glories galore must lie for the picking beyond the hills on the fifteenth.

And when we found out... the wonder and glory and laughter were there, and still are. The outing has an elation about it that springs from a singular harmony of individual and day and place. Its glamour still defies the bus, the ubiquitous bike and even more frequent sights of the sea. It's really an instinctive gathering of the clans that must not be mentioned in the same breath with a bank holiday rush from town or city.

It may run vociferous, even ribald. The masculine spirit of the country heart is on a halter, without its bit, in town, for once; and in wit and repartee might be upholding the honours of a clan, or at least showing that its 'art of the country' is superior to all others.

There would appear to be an affinity between the reasons and healthy instincts which draw people to an annual circus and those which call the countryman to the same seaside place every year. Maybe the infrequency of the visits avoids the risk of one's being bored with seeing the same spot year after year.

Other reasons, like expense, are obvious; but excursions to faraway places on this day have a lonely feeling. Flouting town convention is never the same fun. The countryman might be missing that air of pageantry which ever escorts him, even though he wears flannels while his sister powders and paints her nails.

Keep your novelty and your aped sophistication and give him the clans, the familiar faces in the familiar places where everyone understands his free whoops of glee and every man's your friend in the heel of the evening.

Today, the real assembly point is in either of our towns, Newry or Dundalk. In Dundalk, you see buses crammed with people as tightly as feathers in a pillow. During the war, the real old spirit returned when they brought out discarded brakes and the countrymen found the lost 'Yeh – wheeoo!' of their whoopings.

And, as now, townspeople stood by, trying to be supercilious and aloof from the infectious gaiety and humour of country cousins as they whooped traditional catchwords of the day's outing and, generally, flouted a much-faked sedate convention without being indecorous.

'When a fella's out... let him be out!'

'Pawn yer oul' coat an' come on!'

It is make-believe; a puckish spirit. Half of them at least know the ways of towns and cities in Britain and America.

In either of our resorts the scene still makes a breathless moment as you see the mass of people. Every generation is still there. Last time I was in the Rocks I saw a woman who had closed the gap on the hundredth year. You see them sitting along the sea walls, standing in knots on the street, jaywalking and loitering as cars toot and writhe through them.

You see the solid navy blue of that stolid countryman who still wears his cap with the peak fastener unbuttoned; the old man whose trousers aren't as wide as his grandson's sleeve; but his eye is full of devilry, he believes he has a thirst to be quenched, and his ear is cocked for a whisper of the days that used to be.

The women are in their elements, watching the 'styles'. And unselfconsciously, they stop and stare at some neighbour's daughter.

'I doubt it's all goin' on her back, Biddy!'

'Och well sure – it's the rule now. A big change since the time we were proud *girshes* to come here with a flowery bib an' a few half-hundreds underneath.' This is a reference to a time when shirts, women's underwear and what not were home-made out of half-hundred flour sacks.

They meet a row of girls who greet them happily, and the girls wear their cosmetics well. An old fellow turns on his stick and looks after them. 'A row of mouths,' says he 'like a cat's pad across the concrete from a slaughter house.'

The pubs, of course, are full; the hum of sound from each amply broadcasting the density of the throngs within. A man entertains us in a Synge-like rhythm with his marriage woes and a pithy life history: 'An' look at me now. As continted, sir, as the chile in the creddle, with me round of a loaf, me smell of butther, an odd pull of the pipe, an' me morsel of tay.' Then he stood us a drink. The rhythms of local country speech are delightful.

At a table in the corner, a party that had brought a chicken with them were dining and making a tentative match. Some young people were paraphrasing them.

'Neither lame nor lazy, Packy, *a mhic*!'

'She won't fall in the fire either, *a mhic*. She's long past the day when she'll tear at the pluckin', boy!'

Outside a man was selling blackthorns. He asked half-a-crown, refused ten shillings, and said he could speak in French, German, and Spanish.

'Take the tanner, man –'

'Wouldn't buy the varnish.'

'Yeh grow them yourself, then –'

'No – the Lord grows them!'

And he laughs, hoists one stick like a processional spear, and is lost among the crowds. Outside a dancehall and the amplified wail of jazz, a smiling policeman held back a throng at the door. Wit stabbed back and forward. Once, he patted his baton significantly. Sardonically, jazz could be heard slithering around inside the hall.

Fortunes were told, photographs taken – but not with the best girl: that diverts destiny more potently than a curse, and steers her eventually into another pair of arms. Tea was got, and the waitress teased. And the day wore on, till even the air seemed to weary. Children blubbered as parents hauled them along.

Going home on a sidecar, the jarvey says he drove a party of antiquarians to a place near Kells to see water that will not boil. In the glamour of memory of the day, his tale fell in with the remembered wit, the folklore and fun and tentative play at matchmaking in a glory as old as the hills. The satisfaction of being able to make your own entertainment.

MOUNTAIN FIELDS OF MYSTIC GRAIN

In the plan of fields under the mountain foot the oats had shot into a mist of frothy green with, here and there, the grey-blue lines of the ditches dividing them. And with every moment that passed, the green mist seemed to grow lighter, to rise higher and airily, filling the fields as a milking fills a can, and drowning the ditches under a soft swell of life.

A trick of the wind maybe, but I didn't remind myself. I remembered instead the old man saying: 'The thin stream of milk... The thin blade of corn...' Something seemed to quicken then; a pulse of significance and fantasy startled by the dream of shot oats. Just what the mood was seeking, too; for lit with this touch of awe and fancy, every memory blazed into thought and every thought in turn a symbol, all poised in swift illumination among the imaginative pinnacles of grain magic on the hillsides of Slieve Gullion.

Later that evening I walked the ridge of Garriba towards that plan of fields. The murdering heat of the dry days had gone before a north-east wind, whipping thundercloud across the sky, and the mountain scowled under a gowdy mist cap as ugly as dirty snow. Tall seeding grasses on the lost fields flailed in panic in every gust. Below, the land seemed to mope.

How many times, I wondered, had I watched the first grain from our mountain slopes? I couldn't tell. Ages more than years, it seemed. From every slope of Slieve Gullion I had seen it; from this Garriba, enchanted ridge; from Glen Dhu, bewitched; from Slieve-na-Bola in the moonlight; from Carnagore and the Bohil Breaga in Tiffcrum; from Cloughinnea, mystic ground. And all contributing distinctive moods, it seemed; all like a family line developing turns of character which live as one on the parental heights of Slieve Gullion itself.

And it was worth it. Because in our little cornfields thought and symbol can become as sharply defined as figures in a pageant when the mood is right. Time becomes a myth that is astounding. Already the mountain scowls, and hisses now as winds scurry through heather and whin. But here the grains nod and sway in sage, confident mystery, making the old melody. Here the oats have shot. But there looms colourful wilderness and – death. Nothing seems inanimate now; not even the wild rocks and the tamed ditches; the wilderness or the oats. Each is taking sides with two spirits already braced for combat.

Until the oats shot in jubilation, one saw the massive spread of mountain. Then the corn rises; and then it shoots. And as if it had been secretly preparing, there might be cries of challenge in the air. That crumbled ditch where bracken marches through may mingle with the rocks it came from, but the others stand, no longer grim and accidental memorials to an ancestral grit; they are veins still beating with the purpose that opened the lap and breasts of hill and mountain to corn life. Now, it seems, the fields of the plan strike a positive challenge like spearheads on a war map, thrusting back again into the wild heart of the mountain.

Pageant or poetic fancy? I couldn't say. It had gentler thrills too: the queer and fascinating ache of triumphant loneliness which hangs about last fields. Or was it the mood that saw it as being lonely? For to ponder on the very sight of mountain fields of grain can lead thought to memory like door after door opening to a riot of harvest chord and colour for the children of the mind...

It was dusk as I walked back along the mountain ridge. Now I was crossing some lost fields. The ache that hangs about the whins and heather on lost fields when harvest presence stirs the air... And yet, across Monribba Bog a few fields marooned by heather and whin stood out on the shoulder of the hill in wistful magnificence. Banners they might have been, abandoned in the flight towards the victory of homesteads on wide, flat acres below and beyond the hills: the glory of a people surviving to reclaim their heritage.

I knew that; and yet… the lost fields. Once, they had elated someone's eyes with the promise and fulfilment of ripening grain. Someone cut a *cailleach* there and carried it home in a ritual of triumph. Home… harvest. Dramatic words which, linked together, breathe a holy breath with the aroma of spiritual incense.

I looked towards Cloughinnea on my right, and the dance of the fields up the breast of Slieve Gullion. How innocently, like children asleep, the cornfields lay in that shelter beneath… How snug the white houses. But my eyes could still follow the veins of ditches to where they knotted here and there in the blobs of old walls and a lurching gable. Harvest… home…

I walked on.

And then I was aware of the strange light; a fugitive gleam from the vanishing day which kindled a glow seemingly from within the earth, as it might come from a shoal of fish in a calm, evening sea; a pearled light lingering around the mountain foot and the thrust of fields. Beyond, the land still glowered. Only the chapel belfry in Dromintee had seen this witchery of afterglow that made grass supernaturally green, and heather and rock and cushion of moss so vivid and pure that they became airy and fantastic, almost alarming.

Fantasy danced back again, though reality cried for a hearing in the hiss of heather winds. But the glow kept spreading, billowing it seemed. The cornfields were rehearsing their own pageant of harvest under capes of gauzy green silver and no other dream seemed to matter.

HARVEST TOKENS ON A KITCHEN DRESSER

In the wake-house they had reached me the customary new clay pipe from off a plate, and I had touched my cap and said from my heart: 'Lord 'a' mercy on him.' He had been a friend and an all-round decent man, a storyteller too, and the first man I had worked for in the fields. I had come to look on him as a kind of folk symbol.

I didn't want to go to such a wake; but custom and respect demanded that I should.

Talk among the men in the kitchen of a wake-house always fades when a newcomer enters. It had done so for me, and then slowly began again: talk of work and this and that, neither solemn nor too sober. I sat near the door on the edge of a plank that had been laid from chair to chair to provide extra seating.

I tried not to think of him, but to listen and to join – however selfconsciously – in the talk and light-hearted crack. But the moment my glance went to the top of the dresser, the talk around me seemed to fade. All mental instinct seemed to stop, to change gear as it were; and to adjust itself to a pageant of harvest memory spent in the fields with this man. It led from fantasy to reality and reality, in turn, to the dignity of every harvestman personified...

Over the edge of the top of the dresser I saw the point of his sharpening-stone; next to it his old harvest hat, and at the end nearest the door, just above me, his *cailleach* from last year's grain, the straw and oats drooping in a gentle arc like the neck and head of a dead swan.

I used sometimes to see the *cailleach* hanging over the edge of a picture, with his cap on the other side as if to maintain a balance. But whether by design of custom or casual accident, when harvest approached the *cailleach* was there over the edge of the dresser and facing the door.

Suddenly I realised that, often as I had worked with him, I had never actually seen him plait and cut a *cailleach* in the cornfields. I wondered why... was it that a revered custom, nurtured by instinct, must live by stealth when a new age derides ignorantly? Folk belief apart, an eternal symbol of life is also entwined in the straws and grain of a corn *cailleach* – in every land, where they have or had their own versions similar to ours; and it seems that if man is ever futile enough to pretend to forget it, some innate pulse will impel him to create another.

...The roots of grass still sleep under the busiest city street, weeds and all...

His sharpening-stone next held my eye and mind. I remembered harvest mornings when we had gone to open round the ditches to allow a reaper to work – he to mow with the scythe, I to lift and tie the sheaves. Halfway up the loanan he would halt on his foot, half-turn about, slap his hip and side pockets. 'Ah, dammit to hell! The bleddy sharpenin'-stone. I left it I think at me hand but – will you go back or will I?'

He always forgot and I always went back for it. He was an easy man to work for ('What's the use in takin' the last hair outa the tail?') and sometime during the day as we took a rest and a smoke he would recall the lore of harvest, or tell a story of the days when he went 'up the road' into Co. Louth, where wages were good, and where, anyhow, the harvest came in earlier than around Slieve Gullion; tales, too, of the hiring of harvest help at Peter O'Hagan's pub near Kilcurry, or at Gartlan's house, where the poet Peadar O'Doirnin (buried in Urney beyond Forkhill) made his song 'The Garron Ban'. Apart from these few annual travels (and once when, as a boy, he had been hired in Co. Down by a man of a religious sect he called the 'Seekers'; he used tell how he imagined he was 'being sought instead of the Lord' and fled in the night!) he had never left the valley except to go to fair or market in Newry or Dundalk , Camlough, Newtown or Crossmaglen. Yet his talk had more of the grip of real adventure, wonderfully observed and narrated, than the bragging boasts of men who had had to sleep in sacks at harvest in the Fens of England, their sickles sheathed in scarfs to evade a law which directed that they be in a scabbard.

He called a spade a spade and every beggarman 'sir'. His wit was both traditional and creative and he knew that only humour was kind. One morning, on our way to the harvest field, we met two tramps, a man and a woman. He stopped and leaned on his scythe as if awaiting a close friend. We had a traditional and jocular phrase, used on both courting and married couples, and he used it on the woman: 'Are yous long goin' together?' To which she replied: 'No. We're married by the mile and can divorce at any crossroads.' Of this reply he made a cameo which he fitted into the subtle undertones and exchanges of country speech current in that day, which though told before youngsters, were, like folktales, aimed primarily at the adult mind. He never told a dirty tale, yet many of his stories were so earthy as to be almost risqué today, but even these he would relate safely and with assurance to a famous local reverend DD.

A creative and intelligent man who could neither read nor write, he seemed to be above and beyond the stresses and impulses which disturbed the rest of us: neither greed nor envy could have touched him, and he always talked of wages, money and his own or someone else's house and produce of the land as 'a share of the world' and was quite content with his own.

I remembered that; and remembered that he always seemed to have a cameo or tale each time he stopped to sharpen his scythe in the harvest field – as if the rhythmic swipe of the stone on the blade, and the bent stance in closer adulation to earth, had refreshed his mind. Looking at that stone I remembered how he used sharpen his scythe in the dusk in readiness for the morning, and said that this overnight keenness helped the blade 'to carry the edge'.

But that sharpening was partly habitual, partly a ritual. The stone itself was cumbersome and old, as the harvest hat beside it on the dresser was old as well. Wearing the hat was another kind of instinctive ritual: it became almost an emblem. He always wore a cap to Mass and market, so the hat was surely a discard by someone else – but who? I wished then I had only known: it seemed important.

In style and fit it was outsize, the ribbon-band frayed, the felt showing holes which might have been nibbled by mice. Other old men liked to turn up the rim at the back to over-cap the crown, but he just wore it as it was; and even that was important in some mysterious way. Where he kept it during the rest of the year I never knew. But while he might begin a harvest wearing a cap, he always exchanged his head-dress for the hat after the first dinner-time; and from then until harvest was over it went on top of the dresser… and then disappeared.

Even from the top of the dresser in the wake-house it seemed to contain more breath of his character than can come alive from the individual twists and shapes of a familiar boot.

This trilogy of hat and stone and corn *cailleach* were in correct order, in proper company; like the plaited straws of the *cailleach* itself, each intertwined so much of the man and his personality as I remembered him. The *cailleach* with its heads of grain held the living seed of true life in fact and symbol both: but I thought it odd that I should never have noted before how it hung there like the neck of a dead swan.

…But this was his wake… Swans, I remembered, used come to the bog below the house when the harvest was over, or when the stooks and sheaves from the fields had been hauled home to the haggard near the house and built into snug, rush-thatched stacks, set on butts of stones and green whins. Some people didn't like to see the swans come to the bog: swans were an omen of death. Tales, like that of the Children of Lir being turned into swans, had gone from folk repertoire into a child's schoolbooks. Yet they had other tales of people having been changed into swans, so that the omen itself may have been a lone impression of the symbolic essence of all that remained: dead beauties sacrificed – like the pagan spirit of the *cailleach* itself – on a hearthstone of neglect or an altar of scorn.

In itself the custom of cutting the *cailleach* originally signified a sacrifice, a trapping of the harvest spirit; and in our day a kind of emblem of a *feis* of plenty. Some people actually mixed the oats from the head into the seed of the following spring, so that it had motifs of fertility and reincarnation as well as obeisance to the god of the grain, and, perhaps indicatively, a female at that.

Apart from primordial origin, the very form of the *cailleach* over the dresser, almost alive in its three-stranded plait, had a sense of beauty which seemed to draw out the colour, the tones and temperaments and dramatic lights of every harvest: of back generations of our people entwined in their destinies – back to Mitchel of Newry in the Famine crying 'Hold the harvest! Hold the harvest!' – stretching back from the eternal seed of the grain of the *cailleach* itself to the first fibres of the human race.

This was fantasy escaping from the valid magic of the harvest field into the suppressed mood of a wake in his kitchen, where the rise and fall and swing of the talk replaced the sway and chattering jostle of growing oats. It was more now than poetic fantasy; for, sharpened by human death, it had the reality of a religious sense of ceremony not far removed from the impulses of the pagan myth of the *cailleach*.

But still fantasy… Fantasy pondering the latent awe in each head of grain till the imponderable essence and meaning of it all brought a feeling that quickened the pulse of thought and image with a sensation of glow, as a ripening field itself can glow in the abandoned lights of a harvest dusk – lights like elusive spirits reluctant to desert the pull of a strange and potent presence. You never talked or tried to discuss this presence; but you remember how harvesters, like the man in his shroud in the room, spoke then only in hushed tones.

Remembering that, the thought revealed a new dignity about the dead harvestman. He was at one with the grain in that *cailleach*, dead yet alive; within him lay the core of men gone, more to follow. A majesty seemed to gather about the spirit and image of man moving among the stooks of his harvest fields, and the harmony of the tread to the mystic beat of earth and the throb of grain had a power that thrilled and frightened at once.

All this was kin to the harvest fantasy I had known recurrently for years. In spring the world is young and in harvest young again, when the airs, like an incense lit by the flame of ripening fields, sweeten the mood at every turn and flash of the imagination. It could believe that all life was young and sweet and wonderful: could even see man being one again in harkening to the miracle of earth and seed and fruitfulness, seasoned by the satisfaction of limbs pleasantly wearied by harvest labour, remembering the burnished lights among the stubbles and the chill kiss of dew...

It could, and can, be a shock then to realise that primitive man still walks within our shadows, dogged and real, and not only in the symbol-twist of straw in a corn *cailleach*. Yet for evil or good, man's twin tread in the fantasy and reality of the world of the harvest field has the impact of epic... We fail to listen to that twin step only at our peril.

...The sharpening-stone, the harvest hat, his last *cailleach*... I looked up again and for a moment they seemed to fuse into a representation mightier even than their own individual or even intertwined power of symbol. A decent, unlettered man of integrity on a small mountainy farm stood out suddenly as a king among men in a society where such royalty was common.

When fantasy faded the talk around me in the wake-house merely mimicked a breeze jostling the ripening heads of grain. Outside in the night airs the grain growing in his fields was hardening fast to make that sound he used call 'the cockle rattle': a whispering symphony that can have for the mind and ear the same imaginative fascination which the surf on the shore has for the eye and mind – same sound, same rhythm, same mystery.

But the grain field holds the power of greater thrill. Like some other men, he too could stand and admire a 'piece of oats' and say so; or stand and stare and say nothing. He didn't need to – as at such moments no one really does: there is only room for the impressions and none for the effort of thought that makes for talk.

He was of a community where the mystery of life is fulfilled in preparation for the greater mystery of death: without morbidity, without fear or sentiment, but in a natural, almost impersonal kind of way. Everything about and by him had a hand in all that: like the *cailleach* hanging over the edge of the dresser, now more than ever a symbol of death after the triumph, fulfilment and achievement of life everlasting.

On a minor level of symbol was the ascending tobacco smoke from the fresh clay pipe: symbol, salute – and prayer in one.

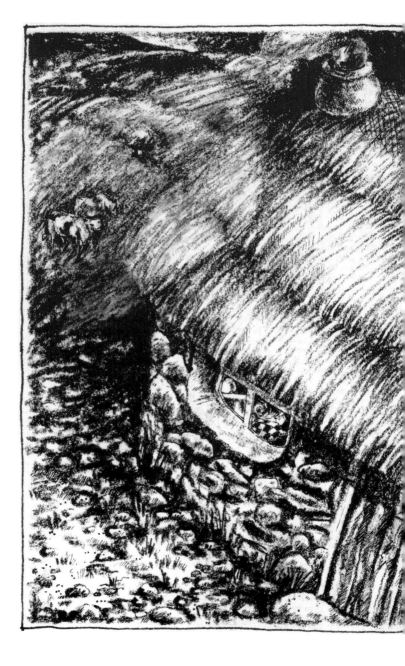

THE HUCKSTER SHOP

Annie's house was low and thatched, crushed between the country road and the foot of a South Armagh hill like a limestone slab in the butt of a ditch. More than a huckster, her shop was an institution that defied the strangulation of rationing red tape until well into the war years.

I can still feel the atmosphere. The key mood in 'Annie's' on Saturday nights was her own morose silence tickled by the deferential whisperings of the customers. It was almost a rural ritual. Rain, hail or snow, you always found the same individuals there – barring death, a cow calving, a returned American, or 'sitting up with a sow' intervened. Each was in his appointed place, always wearing the same clothes ('What's up? What's the good clothes on for?'), always seeming to say the same things.

Her chimney, too, always seemed to smoke, filling the kitchen from the mantelpiece to the rafters; when a man stood up he was a mountain with his head buried in fog.

Even the shadows in her huckster shop had personality. In widening columns they leaned away from tin boxes, cakes of soap, and an alarm clock with a galloping tick on the mantelpiece. Dripping out of the smoke canopy was an especial shadow which I always looked for. It was the shadow cast by the strap and buckle hanging from a pony-collar on the brace; in some secret draught it mocked a long departed wag-of-the-wall.

Behind Annie herself was the window, little more than a foot square, the sash lined with spools of thread, a cocoa tin, and flanked by a half-plucked card of Someone's Powders, boasting as many cures as Diancecht's porridge.

On the edge of the hearthstone Annie sat in a low wicker

chair. She always wore a black apron, drawn taut by her knees, a black shoulder-shawl, and a woollen cap over her fine, white hair. And she was always twirling her thumbs. But her voice was clear and commanding and as hard as the hammers of hell.

Significantly one remembers mostly the dark nights one went to Annie's... when over Glen Dhu, as over a fanlight on a door, rainclouds cavorted in the glare of the hidden lights of Dundalk like hordes of witches in long, loose gowns, leaping in an arc of illumination that shifted, swelled, drew in, but never totally disappeared. You whistled going down her street to the doorway.

Inside you stood with bent head trying to identify the figures. Some sat on the edge of the table; others sat on the settlebed beside and between terraced pyramids of loaves. 'Residenters' only sat on chairs because they were 'making a ceilidh of it', while some young boys sat on the hobs on either side of the fire.

I usually went with a companion, who always left the door open – deliberately. 'Were you reared in a field or what?' she would cry. 'If the mason left a hole there, the carpenter plugged it.'

'There was no door on the house I was in last, Annie,' he would say.

We stood. The silence fell. Someone leaned from the table and murmured: 'What's it doin' outside?'

'Black down dark... Black as your boot...'

'Tryin' hard to rain all day. Ah well... it's the time of year for it...'

Someone else on the settlebed was usually half-bent towards the firelight trying to read the local paper. When you didn't sit she would say: 'Find a seat for yourself.'

'Sure I'm bigger standin', Annie, like a cat sittin'.'

'If your hurry's that big, what took you here?'

If we were in a hurry, we told her. Instantly there was a stir like a breeze among the thicket of shadows. Some lad on the hob was always first with his litany: 'An' I want a loaf, two baps, black an' brown blackenin' an' tobacco for me Da – an' me Ma'll pay you the morra comin' from second Mass, Annie...'

Coins were chirruping in calloused hands held close to bent heads. Fingers probed and accounted.

'An ounce for me when you're at it, Annie...'

'A gallon of oil when you get time, Annie...'

'Oh, a quart for us, too, Annie – I forgot.' It was the lad on the hob. Someone always forgot.

'Any matches, Annie – Oh, an' the paper...'

It was self-serve in Annie's. Whoever was nearest the bread gave out what was asked. Someone filled oil from the drum at the door. Someone got the stick of tobacco and began to cut off ounce plugs ('Keep that knife level on the line now, clumper-head').

Then came the reckoning, interspersed with acidy queries about people, children with chin-cough, a christening or a wake, laying hens – or a sudden and arresting cry after a departing customer: 'Hold on out there!'

He came back, naked loaves under his arm. 'What was it you got? Was it two shillins or half-a-crown you give me?' Deferentially the customer reminded her. 'Oh, aye, so it was. Well, what else did you get? Aye, it was the other fellow got the paper an' matches. What odds? What hurry's on you now that you are back? Sit down and give us a while of your crack...'

Sometimes when we came out the last train from Belfast to Dublin was hurtling out of the cutting in Faughil with a metallic howl. We used to stand quietly and watch it, watch the fleeing bubbles of light in the carriages... listen till the Gap of the North seemed to fold and smother light and sound.

It might have been a two-way symbol: the contemptuous spirit of the city fleeing berserk through our lonely mountain valley... or the level of our social yearnings, its bubble lit with hope, being tipped by time from city to city, searching for a satisfying balance.

THE NEW SPADE

It was, they agreed, a hasky day, but powerful for the time of the year and good for getting out the priddies. The three of us were digging them out with spades, gathering at intervals.

All day the wind had blustered under a cloud-packed sky which rolled in butter-paper grey into the east... But after noon the clouds showed octopus arms of light and became saturated with brightness. Now and then the light romped over the hills and turned the bracken as red as a fox, the ditches blue-grey and the mossy hillocks gold. It warmed the fatigued air over the fields and one, thick with flowering gilgown weed, went as yellow as mustard. There was carnival colour in decaying leaf; and the romping light might have been autumn's mellow handshake, in its pageant of farewell, bidding the earth so-long. Towards evening the crows flew off stealthily to the wood nearby as the light faded. Dead priddy stalks chattered and a leaf ticked. Thistledown felt the wind's pluck and vanished over the ditch. We took shelter behind a ditch of whins when the shower broke and, cleaning our hands on our trousers, filled our pipes. The inside of each leg was plastered with clabber to the knee, so a little extra hardly mattered.

'I hope in God,' the old man began, 'that the weather doesn't break. You might as well be on a whale's back as up here around Hollantine... Thon's a bag'll carry away...' And he made to get up as the wind plucked the end of the bag off the bing of priddies. He had been a sailor most of his days.

'Take your smoke, man,' Peadar said. 'It won't do a button of harm to them. The weight of that shower's away be Killeavy, see...' And beyond the hedges with their crimson blur of haw he pointed his pipe stem at the film of the shower. Then, frog-wise, he shot himself further back into the shelter, and one of his knees burst through his trousers. 'I can call an auction anytime,' he laughed, pecking the *sciflogs* of cloth.

'Mine's adrift, too,' chuckled the old man, also pecking cloth. 'You never see the cheap trousers now in Newry market at all, though I mind when you'd get a pair for next to nothin'.' Wisely, he had taken his spade into the shelter and now began to clean it of earth with a bit of slate which he kept in his vest pocket. Elves of his pipe smoke were already diving into the wind.

'A body should sew patches on their knees for the priddy diggin',' Peadar said. 'Mick Ruagh always done that – You knew Mick Ruagh?'

'Wasn't I at school with him, sure. Lord, but he could handle a spade...'

And as they went on to recount events from the career of Mick Ruagh, the sun flashed through the butt of the clouds to make fairy lances of the rain. It was a merry, frivolous rain. A seagull flew into the shower and was turned to gilt... as the priddies lying on the earth in their sets were gilt, flowing away with the dreamy symmetry of late light on dappled waters. As the light romped over the hills again, the sweet-sadness of October soil mystery romped around the mind.

'We had Mick one time when we tried clawin' out the priddies with our hands,' Peadar said amusedly. 'At dinner-time he put his spade on his shoulder an' said that God never intended no man to make a graip of his fingers – an' hard forcin' we had to get him to stay on an' dig instead...'

Mick was a true spadesman, and in his hands surely the spade acted like something bewitched. He never put a foot to it, but sent it behind a stalk with a jabbing fling, made it shudder, and out came the stalk. Flipping out potatoes, he levelled earth in a zigzag pattern back towards his boot, while nudging dead stalks and weeds into his ruler-like row. Then, as if accidentally, his spade clanged against the toe-plate of his boot to knock off clinging mould – and all as fast and as dexterous as the swerving flight of a swallow or a trout in a pool.

He bought a new spade as selectively as another would buy a horse. Jokingly they used to ask him if he took it to bed as well. For the digging, too, he wore an outsize in coats which wouldn't catch him under the oxters when he had to wear it while working. On each knee, the two patches had been sewn. A spade shaft gnaws cloth, so when the patches developed 'kidney trouble', as he would say, he simply had them renewed. He would be upset, too, if he accidentally sliced a potato. He was a craftsman of the spade.

When the shower was over we went back to work, I to gather the potatoes now, the others to dig out the butts. But imagination kept hunting the romping echo that whispered a fugitive content. In other fields mechanical diggers were skiting earth as a terrier tears out a bank. From across the hill a threshing mill hummed, a sweet-sad sound of a song of plenty and a keen for the dying year. Remembering Mick Ruagh one remembered the hibernates who, eager to delay their winter's sojourn in the town poorhouse were glad to dig priddies for a 'meal's meat', a few shillings and a bed in the barn.

And then the light broke, wet as wine; and the mosses on the hillocks, soaked in its magic, seemed to glow from within like elfin domes of green-threaded transparent copper. Above, a rock became a waterfall as the sun flung a dripping gold to the clouds. But the wind kept up. Slowly the feeling of a manifestation of the infinite spread over the western sky; for the wind seemed to tease the clouds to an inflamed scum which lit up like a rainbow-tinted gas to fill the sky now with a sense of illimitable billowing silk.

None of the crows returned. But into the wind-blown sky the plane came, droning from the north towards Shannon no doubt. I watched it till it became a sinking speck, its drone silenced by distance. And into thought came the image of Mick Ruagh, cleaning his spade at the end of a day's digging and clanging it on the ditch to make it ring like a bell, while answering rings chased its echoes through the darkness. Into thought, too, came the lighted chapel and footsteps going to

61

October devotions. And organ song flowed from the dream-chords of their murmurings, their laments for aching limbs and wind-galled faces, retuned mysteriously to a new fling of romance and consummation by the drone of a plane dipping into the fiery splendour of an October west...

I went to gather as if lifting the fruits of a secret philosophy of soil which, sobering the fantasy that lingered from corn harvest moods, whispered a content that was fugitive no longer.

STORM OVER THE HEARTHSTONE

The cold nipped and bit. Like the bog, the very silences seemed to be frozen, too. Every South Armagh hill was in a striped black and white, as if fabulous fingers from some folktale had clawed away the snow.

I was hoping to find old Peadar to hear his talk, and wondering would I find him in bed, wondering what his humour might be. Turning the bend into Balnamadda I saw he was in the house anyway; at least there was a slow rise of smoke from the chimney. The only sign of life and movement anywhere indeed seemed to come from the chimney smoke of the white-washed houses: for there wasn't a soul to be seen on the road.

The road itself was dry, apart from shallow, isolated drifts like spills of salt set for a rough meal on the oft-scoured boards of a deal table... and then abandoned.

From a bush a lone magpie flew silently, but the bird moved in a hovering, laborious kind of flight: against that background of hill and sky the magpie reminded one of the twist and flash of a steel bit boring a metal as dumb as lead.

And the cold was deadly. Storm seemed to be holding a long, malicious breath and the world knew it and was afraid...

Peadar lived alone; and I found him sitting at the fireside airing socks. He was alone – except for the cat. He's a tall, thin, loose-jointed man whose face looks no broader than the gnarled bulk of his two joined fists. He wore a huge moustache and always smoked a clay.

'Well,' I said to him in the usual monosyllable of country greeting to a friend.

'Well,' he said back, 'an' is that yourself?'

Speech seemed to pain him.

There was a set of fan-bellows beside his right hand.

Absentmindedly, and out of habit, he turned the wheel slowly, and the current of air driven through the tiny inbuilt tunnel under the hob began to purr: it roused spurts of flame in a mound of coal slack in the low grate on the hearth.

There were two hobs. On one a sock lay across a twisted, heavy boot with loose stitching showing on the jaws. From the other hob across the fire Peadar's cat opened its eyes when the fire, like the snorts from a caulked gas ring, began to murmur into brightness and flame. And the cat was very bedraggled.

Peadar was far from being a storyteller, but he did have folklore. His moods could be unpredictable and his humours sudden; but he usually found good heart and the right phrase if he felt – or could be induced – to recall the incidents and anecdotes that were the stuff and life of country living before a selfconscious, miscalled 'culture' of urban overlay took hold of the rural mind.

The kitchen was warming now; it was bright in the sound of the fire. But outside the air remained still and grey against the window.

Yet when Peadar spoke it was only to complain about the snow… The air had the feel of more snow, he said… That snow on the hills, too, was only waitin' on more… But sure wasn't it only the time o' year for snow… What could we expect… But that didn't help either at his time o' day, when age pushed the blood far back in a body…

And, as if really camouflaging an effort aimed to restore vigour to his hands, he began to rub the sock between his fingers.

The old clock in its oblong wooden case was on the wall facing him, and facing the window; and it might have muffled its slow ticking, so that it would – as one felt it must do – suddenly stop.

Suddenly, too, Peadar stopped knuckling the sock. He seemed to be staring at the cat – and the cat was staring back. For a sound had boomed down the chimney: a churning thunder of sound which was streaking through cloudy echo-halls in the heavens above the hills.

'God bless us...' Peadar's eyes were now steadily, apprehensively, on mine and alive with query. 'Is that wind?'

It was a jet plane.

In the end even the cat looked up into the sooty throat of the chimney, but with a casual, almost contemptuous curiosity, in a superior way, as if humanly aware of the cause of the anxiety that the sound of the plane had aroused in Peadar. He seemed to be aware of these implications too, for he was staring hard at the cat himself.

I asked him what had happened the cat, for it was so bedraggled and dirty it might have been dipped in glue, the way its fur stuck to its body in close wisps like a medallion of stubby daggers.

'The cat?' said he, and picked up the short clay pipe from the hob. The cat swayed to and fro, now watching the fire of crooked ribs and eyes of flame – the way old *cailleach*s of women used do when they claimed they could read fortunes and the future from the hieroglyphics of embers, or in ashes raked with the fingers: 'reading the rake', as they called it.

'The very divil himself,' Peadar said, 'couldn't put manners on that cat. Leave the kitchen to him an' the minute he has your back turned he's stuck into some harm the same as if he never saw a decent bite. An' look't the wastrel – Look't... *barrdóg*s on him with meat!'

'Why, man alive!' Out went Peader's hand in a wave of self-reproach and the sock in his fist swept past my nose like a bat. 'Man alive, I doubt if he's right betimes.' He meant bewitched, and his voice had accordingly dropped in hoarse awe, as if actually afraid now that the cat could not only hear, but understand what he was saying.

I waited, hopefully, for Peadar to continue. He was warming up. Here was an opening to a vein of folklore and I mentioned – as if trying to remember – a tradition about bewitched cats, especially the famous talking cat of Moyra Castle in our Gap of the North.

But Peadar ignored my remark and said: 'I put him out goin' for the pension the day, closed every door an' window – an' there he was, there on that hob when I got back. What d'you think did the flamer do? Fired himself down the bleddy chimley. You couldn't see an eye in he's head for soot when I got home here. An' he didn't leave a smell o' butter on that table; an' gettin' at the milk he be to fall into the crock o' clean well water. It was like a bog hole when I went to make the mouthful o' tay – an' he'll ate cheese! In all your born days did you ever hear tell of a cat that'd ate cheese?'

On the gusty rises of such earnestness and humour it seemed an easy drift into the telling of tales of beliefs about cats; bewitched cats and all the rest.

He drifted instead into memories of the days when a travelling woman – one with her cat – had stayed in the house, hemmed in by snow: making a bed of straw in the corner or across the hearth for themselves – 'on a wisp', as he called it, remarking that women in the labour of childbirth thought it lucky as well to be lifted out onto the same 'wisp', because the Virgin had rested on straw. He recalled another travelling woman who took over the settlebed and made the people 'wait hand an' foot on her' for a week.

Better still, the travelling woman snowbound in my grandfather's on the Dromintee Old Road. She had, of course, her own flour, which she had begged. When given permission to make her own griddle of bread she told my grandfather at the fireside to 'Quit your smokin' an' spittin'' while she was around the hearth, and reminded him that she had 'once owned three cows in the Co. Monaghan'. He was so stunned by such objurgation at his own fireside – and gloomy anyway over the snow – that she felt she had him not only humbled, but cowed. War ensued inevitably, in which even the cat – and the South Armagh spirit of hospitality – fled. Out she had to go into the snowdrifts. Hospitality nevertheless decreed a compromise, via the pleas of my grandmother, that the travelling woman be allowed a sojourn in the barn for a term of hours as chastisement. But this term of probation was reduced when she began to play a tin whistle behind the closed doors, to which his temper danced anew. Local ridicule was feared then, and he saw the gathering throng of spectators on the ten-foot drifts on the road overlooking the wall. The travelling woman was brought back to the house.

Just then Peadar's kitchen darkened. He stopped talking, looked at me, and I saw the heartiness steal from his face. He turned to look out the window.

It was terribly quiet again: the echoes of his voice reminded me somehow of the reverberations of that jet plane.

They might indeed have become ethereal graters. For, like shreddings of the frozen silences, a few snowflakes had begun to glide outside the window.

Peadar turned and crouched over the hearthstone towards the fire and began to moan and make complaints about the cold and the snow.

He would talk no more.

COUNTRY CHRISTMAS EVE

'The dark days of Christmas', which the old people lament about (in a meteorological sense), have come so swiftly that it seems only a day or so since someone asked: 'Well, an' have yeh no word of Christmas with you?' The turkeys have been 'sold and spent'. The marketing has been done. The trappings of mercenary excitement fall like dead leaves; and another less tangible excitement tenderly sustains thought and the spirit on a higher plane. The switchover seems to have left even the hills breathless. A magic unconsciously reverent has filtered through the fibres of thought and spirit, and nothing has physical affinity... 'Everything exists, everything is true, and the earth is only a little dust under our feet.'

One loves the wholesome atmosphere of the walk to the village. A new insight seems to find meaning in inanimate things and tenderness in everything. Thought has the airiness of dreaming, detached from the process of conception. And all, even the expectation of friends in the pub beyond, is part of a spiritual symmetry where existence is etched in toil, tears and hoping.

The road here hoists itself over a thrust of the mountain into the starlight, twists past a bullet-gouged gable and down through the bog, crouching till it pushes over another hill, and rushing with a sweep into the village. The hills are swathed in starlight and an abandoned afterglow of evening.

One pauses to stare. Reponse, a mysterious chord like an old piece of music being played far away, stirs in one's heart. Its meaning flutters near comprehension like a butterfly against the pane, seeking light. Heavy footsteps ahead tap on the road; somewhere else there are voices like limping winds. A light sways at the other side of the bog where someone is

71

foddering; it winks, sways, winks again, and is gone. No other lights are sprinkled over the hillsides or valley; and for a moment it saddens to realise why no lighted candles are in the windows tonight. The atmosphere is robbed of a tone as individual as it was precious.

Houses cling to the breast of the hill like sleeping seagulls. Part of the breast swells against the bog. One can see the thumb of the hill which lurches towards the village. Character shows its spouse tonight, an insistent homeliness; and the imagination is welcomed much too warmly. Soundless echoes die at birth and become eternal; echoes for the mind's sight, like a star falling, with the spirit amazed by the star-track. The atmosphere fuses thought, land and starlight; each essence of this symmetry zips open the meteors of existence and salvation... And the spirit smiles, ironically, through the maze of fading star-paths, no older, no more infallible, than its own emotions.

But one can find the emotional essence of this character and homeliness in the men in the village tonight. It is the humble gestures of living that excite the more enduring echoes not to be so easily refuted, out of twilights, by the laws of commercial supply and demand. Does some exile ache tonight when this emotional wonder ushers the spirit among flakes of ferro-concrete pencilling the sky; of sidewalks thronged and silky under neon signs; of glib talking – existing amicably with starlight and hills and voices dribbling *sciflog*s of adage and tradition, like an old hymn? The thrill of it soars above its impossibility for tonight... 'Everything exists, everything is true...'

Below lies the village of Forkhill ('Far-cill', as the older men will say it, taken in Gaelic some think, from the name of an ancient clan, Orcaill, though possibly from *fuar coill,* meaning the cold wood; the famous forest of Dunreavy Wood ended at the village). Mick will be there in the pub, droll, hesitant before uttering a simile alive with imagination. Thomas will shrug his traditional witticisms fittingly, so old that they are new to us. Barney will be there with his creative wit, real and barbed as true wit must be, the sparks of instantaneous fusion of intellect and imagination singeing the words that inspired it. And Thomas will say, and define creative wit in the words of tradition: 'He hasn't to look for he's answer.' All will sing, or else 'leave their stick' on someone else and have them sing in their place.

It is no debauch. The countryman's attitude to the pub differs from that of his city brother. It is no club to him; he does not go out of indispensible habit. On this night only one is sure to meet one's men friends together. When, one wonders, will a Christmas card depict such a scene which inspires so much of the virile countryman?

The mood of Christmas Eve refutes suggestions of any debunking; but depictions of red-coated gentlemen feasting in an inn, coaches bogged in snow, sketches of the Yule log mean little to him. Tales of old Christmases tell of going to the *margadh mór*, the big market day, when the stars were on the sky in the morni ; of cavalcades of creel-laden asses, the women riding, and all singing, returning when the stars were out again.

From these we arose. We can, under pressure of an alien attitude, be ashamed and be shallow; we cannot deny it. From these we go on. I hear someone singing in the pub.